BEEN THERE, DONE THAT?

DO THIS!

An Insider's Guide to Overcoming Your Dysfunctional Past

Written by
Sam Obitz

Foreword by Michelle Craske, Ph.D.

Super Tao, Inc.
P.O. Box 1081
Manhattan Beach, CA 90267

Copyright © 2003 by Sam Obitz
ISBN: 0-9742595-3-5

www.tao3.com

Book Cover by James Cloutier

Edited by Robert Spaeth

Printed in the U.S.A.

Warning-Disclaimer

This book is designed to inspire and help people get started on the road to personal growth through the use of established methods that are derived from Cognitive Behavioral Therapy (CBT). The author feels that the most important step to recovering from a dysfunctional past is getting started with the tools outlined in this book. At the conclusion of this book the author recommends additional resources for further growth.

That said, this book is sold and should be read with the understanding that the publisher and author are not engaged in diagnosing or curing psychiatric conditions. It is strongly recommended that you seek the services of a professional trained in CBT to help you with your journey.

Table of Contents

Section III Un Poquito Mas

Foreword

In a succinct and insightful portrayal, Sam Obitz describes his journey from sufferings of anxiety and depression to his mastery over them. He describes his process of recovery through the skills that he learned in cognitive behavioral therapy; a type of therapy that is considered to be a well researched and effective treatment for anxiety problems. Sam's description of empowering tools of change – of learning to look at things from an objective standpoint and realizing that even the worst can be managed – is an excellent summary of the essential elements to cognitive behavioral therapy, and his descriptions are particularly remarkable because they are from his own perspective – of what he learned and how he changed – which is very different from every other currently available text book description. Sam's story unravels the myth and mystery of therapy, especially as he gives his perspective of his therapists and the experience of having somebody else give him encouragement and advice on how to overcome his own anxiety. This book will be a source of education and inspiration for the many who suffer from anxiety but do not believe that treatment would be effective for them.

Michelle G. Craske, Ph.D.

Professor

UCLA Director

UCLA Anxiety Disorders –

Behavioral Research Program

Acknowledgments

So many people to thank, but so little space... Thus, I'll start with everyone I have ever met, as I would not be who I am today without all of the experiences I have had.

If it were not for many of my friends, I never would have survived long enough to get to the point where I found the tools described in this book and reaped their benefit.

Of course I would be remiss if I did not thank Michelle G. Craske for her support and enthusiasm, as well as all of her research that has benefited so many people, and Matt for personally getting me going on (and introducing me to) the tools outlined in this book.

I would also like to thank my wife who had to live through many years of my suffering with me, and thus suffer considerable pain and confusion of her own as a result.

Though I have never met them, I would

like to thank Albert Ellis, Aaron Beck and David D. Burns (and all the unnamed others) for their work developing and furthering Cognitive Behavioral Therapy (CBT).

My parents, for doing the best they could under the circumstances. Julie for being the little sister I never had, and Phil and Penny for their support, inspiration and friendship, which has been invaluable to me.

Finally, I would like to thank all the people who offered direct help, as well as encouragement, to me on this book. Including but not limited to: JT, Montie & Dyan, RCB, JS, Ken, RS, JC, Gary, RB, Chris, DJ, DM, TAO, DW, Kasey, TP, MS, DF and Donna DeGutis.

Introduction

One of the problems I encountered throughout my therapeutic relationships was that more often than not the person attempting to treat me had never gone through what I was going through. I'm not saying that you have to go through anxiety attacks and depression to be able to help someone out of it, but it certainly can be a huge advantage. There are countless examples of things in life we read and learn about that nothing written ever captures the essence of and we cannot fully understand until we've been there.

The most obvious example of this for me was becoming a parent for the first time. There was no way to conceive of all of the changes you go through emotionally. For me it was EXTREMELY difficult to fathom that my child spitting up on me would not bother me. I used all of my resources to try and conceive how that could even be remotely possible. I mean who knows me better than me? Time and again friends would not just tell me, but assure me that it would not bother me, and sure enough they were right. But there was no way I would have been able to find that out without experiencing it. The whole experience opened up a new world for me. I can't imagine anyone being more afraid of having children than I was. In fact I planned my entire life around not having any out of the fear that I would turn into my father and be a miserable parent. So far I have been wrong, but my thinking was so skewed going into it that I was able to come up with volumes of disconfirming evidence whenever people assured me that I would be a good parent, that I was convinced that I would be a bad parent. It was all in my head and the result of negative thinking patterns that were formed growing up that no longer serve me.

Part of the problem of being depressed is that you are keeping bad patterns of thinking you grew up with alive (the ones you needed to survive) because they feel comfortable to you; when in fact they're what are keeping you depressed. It's not unlike having a normal route to get to work that you have traveled for five years that takes you half an hour. Then they put in a new highway that can get you there in 15-minutes but you refuse to try it because it's different. Once you get out of your comfort zone (which no longer serves you well anyway) you can begin to make the changes in your thinking that will lead you to changes in your life that lead you to happiness. You will be amazed how quickly you begin to see benefits and that heavy burden of sadness is lifted from your shoulders.

Why am I telling you all this? Because I have now seen both sides and I can assure you that these steps, which may seem simplistic, work where everything else you have tried has failed.

Section I Background

Chapter
1

The Un-level Playing Field

Today more than ever we are living in a society full of dysfunctional families. Fewer and fewer of us are being raised in loving supportive families that prepare us to thrive and be happy once we leave them. Many of us are not even aware of all the disadvantages we are saddled with as they are often things that are not easy to quantify. Not having a car is easy to quantify. Not having been brought up with a solid foundation from which to grow and flourish is not so easy to see.

Although it is hard to quantify what exactly makes up a solid foundation, it usually would involve a family in which you knew you were unconditionally loved – ideally by both parents – and knew that they would always love you no matter what. It includes having parents who supported your need to explore and encouraged you in whatever your interests were, who also taught you right from wrong and taught you to have respect for yourself and others.

My childhood was not blessed by such a solid foundation. My mother died when I was three years old, leaving me to be raised by my father who was 59 years old at the time. In my family I was liked – not loved – only as long as I didn't upset my father – which was about 5% of the time – as he would seemingly go out of his way to find reasons to be upset with me. He encouraged me to do whatever **he** wanted me to do and discouraged me from doing most other things. Everything in my family was predicated on fear rather than support. My father blamed me for everything and took every shred of self-respect out of me as he constantly berated me. He also discouraged any exploration and made me feel like I was a bother to him.

Whether your upbringing was more or less severe than mine, perhaps you too have a multitude of developmental problems that, left unchallenged, can be roadblocks to your happiness and or success. To complicate matters we are often completely oblivious to most if not all of the destructive thinking patterns we have that are holding us back. The good news is that once you are finished with this book you will have the tools you need, that when practiced can lead to a revolutionary change in the way you think, feel and live.

Growing up we can see when a friend drives up in a car how fortunate that friend is to have a car. It is not uncommon for friends to be jealous of their friends who have cars and to want a car of their own. Now on the other hand if a friend shows up who has a solid foundation; that is not readily apparent. Since you are not aware of your friend's solid foundation you are not likely to be jealous and want a solid foundation of your own.

In other words, people who grow up in dysfunctional families often do not know what they have missed out on, especially in terms of support and their development as human beings. This often causes them to feel that something is wrong with them when they struggle with the things that come naturally to all of their friends who happen to have solid foundations. We never consider, much less realize that we are not playing on a level playing field with our peers.

It is as if we are forced to build our house out of whatever scraps we could find and are disappointed with our end result. Our peers build beautiful houses that we envy. We can't figure out how they do it because we are unaware that they have all the finest tools and materials available to them. It was not that anything was wrong with us, we just didn't have the availability of the same tools and supplies.

This would be like having a one-mile race with a friend and it takes him about two minutes to finish the race and you take just over four minutes to finish. The obvious conclusion would be that your friend is almost twice as good as you at racing. What was not apparent was that your friend was in a car and raced to the finish line in it, while you were forced to run the whole way. Now would you conclude that the guy in the car is the better athlete because he won the race? Of course not, but that's what people from dysfunctional families conclude when their performance does not measure up, because they cannot see all of the advantages they have missed out on. We often wonder why it is so easy for others to accomplish things because we cannot see much less conceive of, all the support they have that we do not.

It is not at all uncommon for us to see ourselves (quite often accurately) as smarter and more able than those around us making it all the more frustrating as we watch others achieve while we are struggling so hard. This only serves to make us feel worse as we begin to beat ourselves up with such thoughts/ internal dialogue as: "Something must be wrong with me; I'm smarter and more able than "blank", but "blank" always out performs me." It becomes a vicious circle that seems harder and harder to get out of as time goes by, but it's not, as I will show you how many people have overcome their circumstances in the upcoming chapters.

Chapter
2

Survival Skills

Survival skills: What you learned growing up is what is holding you back now...

Growing up in an unhealthy and/or volatile situation/family forces you to come up with skills that enable you to live through your situation. These skills are essential for you to survive. Unfortunately, once you leave the family/situation, these skills are no longer useful and in fact are quite likely to hold you back from achieving what you are capable of achieving. We often dream of what life will be like once we are free of our dysfunctional families but after the initial excitement from physically breaking free wears off, we often find ourselves stuck in the same negative patterns.

Why does this happen? The reason for this is the majority of our life we focused on developing survival skills and though we no longer need them, it is often all we have. They are so ingrained that we do not even realize they are there and we are keeping the problems we had growing up alive by repeating the same patterns or behaviors. Though we are physically free, we are imprisoned by our minds, usually without even knowing it.

The way we react to things that happen to us in our daily lives is colored by our past even though the past is no longer relevant in our lives. We learned to deal with everything from a survivalist's point of view and not only is there no longer a need to look at things from that point of view, it is usually destructive to our lives. Once we are physically free from the family/situation that caused us our pain and forced us to learn these survival techniques, it is only our improper processing of what happens to us in our daily lives that keeps us miserable.

Unfortunately most of us are unaware of this and even if we are aware of it we do not have the tools to deal with this problem. I saw umpteen different psychologists and psychiatrists in the last 25-years and it was not until a couple of years ago that I finally found someone in a research program that gave me the tools I needed to help myself. For 25 years I was busy thinking I was so damaged that I could never experience happiness. In fact I was starting to develop some pretty impressive arguments as to why nothing would work for me.

This is not uncommon as nearly everyone who is suffering is convinced that they are the one person in the world who is beyond hope. They all sincerely think, "but I'm different." You are not different, the fact that you think you are unfixable is simply one of the most tell-tale signs/symptoms that proves you are suffering and in need of help.

Many have spent years in and out of therapy with little to show for it, reinforcing their conviction that they are the **one person** who is permanently damaged. In fact, there's a high likelihood that you feel that way right now. I'm happy to inform you, that you, and all the rest of them are mistaken.

I went through several therapists during that time and they all focused on getting me to express my feelings and talk about my past and present struggles. I'm not saying that this was a complete waste of time, but I believe that you reach the law of diminishing returns rather quickly in this form of therapy. It was not until I met a young therapist in training (named Matt) who forced me to focus on how I was thinking about things rather than getting the hurt out, that I began to experience concrete positive changes in my life. After just three sessions with him I was already noticing the most significant improvements I had ever experienced in my life. But I'm getting a little ahead of myself....

Chapter
3

Changing Your Future

Matt showed me that I could change my future, but not my past. Therein lies the secret to getting better and learning to enjoy what life has to offer. This was obvious, yet it had never occurred to me, or any of the people in the group who were suffering. Most of the therapists I had seen wanted to focus on my past and get me to talk through my past. I'm not saying that there is no use for this; in fact the release often makes you feel good in the short term, but it does not help change the mechanisms in place that are holding you back. While it may "feel" good to talk through your past, it does not give you the tools you need to change the warped way of looking at things that you developed to survive your past, and that no longer serve you well.

Therefore once the relief wears off you are left no better off than when you arrived. Contrarily, when you are taught the tools which I will be discussing in upcoming chapters, you will have something to use that will help you lift your blue moods on your own. This not only will make you feel better at any given time but also, because you are helping yourself, you will receive the added benefit of building your self-esteem, which will further help you get on down the road to lasting happiness.

I talked about my past for years and years and years, with several different therapists and though I made some progress, very little of it was lasting and I would always end up needing to go back for more sessions. I met many people who were in therapy for long periods of time and never seemed to be making any progress (what I began to call "Therapist Junkies"). I desperately did not want to become a Therapist Junkie.

That's why I had so many stops and starts in my therapy history. I would get so down that I would need to go back, but I experienced the law of diminishing returns within a few months each time. Out of habit and fear of falling back, I would continue to go for years at a time before taking a break. There is nothing like a mirror to help you see things clearly. I would see friends that were Therapist Junkies and they looked so pathetic that I would then realize I was either there myself or on my way there again and get out.

Unfortunately I was still stuck without much relief or any skills to take me forward and help me not need to go back into therapy. I hated therapy after awhile and hated myself even more for needing to go back again and again. It was a vicious circle that devoured my self-esteem and I was becoming convinced that I would never get better and I was close to being so worn down I was ready to give up.

Chapter
4

The Turning Point

I had reached a new bottom and it was hard to imagine it could get any worse. I was having insomnia, depression and the most compelling suicidal impulses and thoughts I had ever had. It made me wonder which came first? Did the insomnia cause the depression or did the depression cause the insomnia? I never figured that one out, but what I did find out was that the two together had a synergistic negative force that was unparalleled in my experience.

I had suicidal thoughts since early in my childhood, but this was the only time I had them combined with the compulsion to act on them. It was terrifying to me because even during that horrific time, I knew I didn't want to commit suicide, but the thoughts and feelings were so overwhelming I was afraid that I would do it. I knew it only took an instant to act on those horrible feelings and (especially) in the middle of the nights when I had the insomnia I was desperate to escape the pain. Keeping sight of the fact that I wanted to live, during those times, was one of the hardest things I have ever done and it was getting harder each day.

I was so desperate for help that I finally let go of my need to appear "normal." I confided in my friend Gary that I was really struggling and wanted to meet his friend –Chris – who he had told me was a nationally recognized child psychologist. We arranged to meet in a bar in Santa Monica, CA one evening. Gary and I arrived first and visited for awhile as Chris was running late. I never let on to Gary just how desperate I was, but I was feeling like I was close to my wits' end.

When Chris arrived the three of us visited for a few minutes after introductions, then Gary excused himself to go to a Laker game and Chris and I talked for over an hour.

He was a great listener and I believe he sensed my desperation. When we were finished talking he gave me the name of a colleague at UCLA who was conducting a number of studies on panic and anxiety, which he thought might be of help to me.

Ironically, the person he referred me to was a woman my psychiatrist from college had told me about years earlier, who had come up with some ground breaking treatments for panic and anxiety in her work at State University at New York. I called and spoke with her and she took my name and phone number and said that someone from the program would be contacting me to see which study was the best fit for me.

When I received that call I was asked several preliminary questions and then told that there would be an intake interview that would take two to four hours to complete. A few days later Brian called and we scheduled a block of four hours to meet and we ended up going over the allotted time and had to meet again for three more hours to complete the intake interview. When we completed the interview Brian told me that he felt I was qualified for a couple of the studies but he had to go over my intake interview with a supervisor before it was determined which group I would be a part of.

I didn't fully realize how down I was until the study had concluded 12-weeks later and Brian called to schedule the same interview post treatment. He scheduled three hours this time and said if we didn't finish in that time we could do the rest over the phone. I met Brian at noon for the interview and we were done by 12:40pm. Both he and I were amazed by the difference. He even said based on the way I answered the questions I would no longer be classified as depressed. Even on my best days when I was as happy as I thought I could be prior to the group-study I would ALWAYS fall into the depressed category on those inventories; the only question would be to what degree I was depressed! My interviews with Brian at the 6-months post treatment and 12-months post treatment had the same positive result as the immediate post treatment as well.

Several weeks later I was called and told I would be entering a group study run by Matt and Gregorei that focused on panic disorder. It was to consist of twelve weekly group meetings and also included six individual meetings with a therapist to be assigned to each group member. The individual sessions were focused on general depression rather than panic disorder.

Before we met as a group each individual in the group had to fill out a bunch of paperwork to get a reading of where each one of us was at psychologically at the beginning of the group and undergo some Behavioral Assessment Testing (BATS). While we were each doing this Gregorei was conferring with everyone in the group to figure out what time would be best to have the group meetings.

Chapter
5

The Big Day

When the day finally came for our first meeting I was hopeful and skeptical at the same time. It was hard to imagine that after years of therapy with many respected psychotherapists to little avail, that 12-weeks with some wanna-be therapists in a group setting was going to be any different. By the time Gregorei and Matt came to get us in the waiting room we had all introduced ourselves. Much to my surprise two of the people in the group knew each other already

My first impression of Gregorei was that he seemed very rigid and methodical. Matt initially struck me as being high strung, very motivated and looked like he stepped out of an MTV rock video. They covered a lot of material in the first couple of sessions, and though I was still hopeful, I would be lying if I said I had much faith that what they were teaching us was going to work for any of us and certainly not for me (probably just like you are thinking as you read this, everyone in our group was convinced that they were the ONE person beyond repair).

Things really started to change for me after my second individual appointment and our fourth group meeting. I was pleasantly surprised to be assigned to Matt for my individual therapist. Matt had several surprising qualities that were not readily apparent at first glance. More than any therapist I had ever been associated with, Matt made you feel like he wanted you to succeed (a trait shared by most exceptional teachers and coaches) and you in turn didn't want to let him down. He was often incredulous with the way I would beat myself up over minutia and it was through his genuine disbelief and astonishment that I could see the folly in my ways of thinking.

Matt also had a great sense of how much each of us could handle and how best to get through to each of us. By the last few sessions I marveled at his ability to listen and pick his spots. One member of our group had so much of her life tied up in her depression I didn't think there was any way that Matt could get through to her. I was amazed at how far he would let her go on before bringing her back to what mattered. It was always much longer than he would let the rest of the group go on. But it was what he needed to do to get through to HER.

I was struggling with the exercise that I now believe is the most important exercise of all that I will outline later in this book; What Matt and Gregorei called the Thought Tracking Form, though I prefer to call it the Thought-Error-Analysis or TEA form. On the surface it seemed incredibly simple but for some reason every time I sat down to do it I would freeze up and could not do it. I would later realize that the reason I had so much difficulty with it was because it was a Catch-22 situation for me. My perfectionistic thinking and fear of failing at the exercise was getting in the way doing the exercise. I felt like I would be able to do this exercise when I got better, but what I needed to do was **this exercise** to get better.

Consequently, I was beating myself up because I was feeling like an idiot for not being able to do such a simple exercise and expressed my frustration to Matt in one of our individual sessions. Matt told me to quit being so hard on myself and pointed out that this exercise is in fact difficult, especially for someone who is depressed. It had never dawned on me that what appeared so simple could in fact be difficult and that it did not have to be done perfectly the first time for it to be effective. I still struggled with it and felt a lot of resistance toward the exercise, but as Matt promised it got easier to do over time and I'm still doing it to this day.

Meanwhile Gregorei seemed like the strict disciplinarian who was going to slap us on our hands if we didn't do all of our homework each week. He spoke with a strong Eastern European accent and he would have made a great drill sergeant. I say this affectionately as I thankfully can still hear myself repeating the words "the physical symptoms are not dangerous" in his voice and accent whenever I feel anxious.

As I mentioned previously, another thing that separated Matt from other therapists I have seen is that he had suffered panic attacks before. That gave him a lot more credibility in my eyes. With my apologies to male OB/GYN doctors; if I wanted to learn more about childbirth I would want to talk to a female OB/GYN who has given birth, not a male OB/GYN who was only capable of seeing pregnancy from the outside. I want someone who has seen and experienced the "whole enchilada," as they say.

In fact one of the reasons I decided to write this book was because I had something to bring to bear to the subject that most people that treat anxiety and depression do not have; severe first hand experience of over 30 years. I also decided to make this book short so as to make it less overwhelming to the people who it is designed to help. Lord knows that people who suffer from depression do not need another wordy intimidating book on a cure.

I have been there and experienced this too many times already to do that to you. The key to beating anxiety, depression and gaining your dysfunctional family freedom is to get started and see some real progress in those early steps and that is what this book is designed to do for you. At the end of this book I will point you to additional resources for help once you have had some success trying my recommendations and you are feeling ready for more.

Section II ...Time for a Change

Chapter
6

Learning to Fish

Give me a fish and I will have a nice meal; teach me to fish and I will never go hungry. There in that saying lies the difference between my experience with Matt versus every other therapist I have ever met. My appointments with most therapists were like that one meal of fish, but at my appointments with Matt he was teaching me to fish. The literal difference being that in my sessions with most therapists, I would experience some emotional relief, but at my sessions with Matt I was learning how to give myself relief whenever I needed it. The "Key" tools that Matt gave us I eventually began to call the "Empowering Tools of Change".

The Empowering Tools of Change are some simple methods you can use to change the way you think about things. When you keep your thoughts inside there is no way to test them out to see if you are thinking accurately about things. If you are suffering from anxiety or depression there is an almost 100% likelihood that you are not thinking about things accurately. Once you bring these errors of thought to the light of day, you will be able to refute them and see how ridiculous most of these thoughts that have been keeping you down really are.

Thoughts and feelings are not facts. You may have heard the saying "Feelings are not facts." This is true, but all of your feelings come from thoughts and just because you have a thought does not make the thought a fact. So I prefer to say thoughts are not facts.

If your thinking is inaccurate, then your emotions will be too. For example: If you think coming in last in a race is good you will celebrate when you lose; conversely if you think winning a race is bad you will be discouraged by your victories. All of our emotions come from our thoughts. Emotions always follow thoughts; they are reactions to what we interpret as happy, sad, etc. Whether we feel happy or sad has to do with our interpretation of what we are experiencing, not the experience itself. That is why two people in the exact same situation can feel totally different about their experience.

Just because your parents or teachers or brothers or sisters or even your friends or enemies labeled you as being defective in some way does not mean that the label is accurate. It is like the power of suggestion takes over our minds. Often when a label is affixed to us as we are growing up, we make the mistake of looking for and focusing on any evidence we can find that supports these false labels because we fear they are accurate. This is usually done to the exclusion of overwhelming evidence to the contrary that we neglect to see (the technical term for this would be "Ignoring the Positive"). In many cases we have bought into our labels and are so convinced of their truth that we dismiss any evidence that refutes what we have been labeled as "not counting" or "not being repre-sentative of the real me." David D. Burns, M.D. in his excellent book "Feeling Good" refers to this as the binocular trick, but I like to call it the **reverse binocular trick**.

It's as though we look at every positive thing we do through the wrong side of the binoculars so as to make any accomplish-ment we have made appear miniscule. And look at all of our faults through the proper side of the binoculars to make all of our faults seem huge.

This is all part of the affliction at work against you and bears little or no resem-blance to reality. It seems real in your head and you will continue to believe it is real until you are brave enough to expose these errors of thinking to the light of day where *"even you"* will see the ridiculousness of these thoughts. You will soon see how poorly you have been treating yourself and come to real-ize that if you treated your friends like you treat yourself you wouldn't have any friends. It's no wonder you feel miserable.

Once you begin to do the exercises that make up The Empowering Tools of Change – which I'm about to outline for you over the following five chapters – you will be able to counter these inaccurate thoughts and be on a new path to freedom from the prison in your mind. They will allow you to enhance your existence and your ability to experience true happiness.

Chapter
7

The Empowering Tools of Change – Step One

The first step on the path to freedom and happiness is to familiarize yourself with the most common thinking errors troubled people make. I have listed the four errors that I found to be my biggest offenders, followed by several other thinking errors people make. Once you become familiar with them, you will then need to start recognizing when you are making them and substitute counter thoughts that are more accurate in their place. After each error in thinking, I have provided real examples of each of these errors from my past. They are:

1) JUMPING TO CONCLUSIONS: *This is where you overestimate the likelihood that a negative event is going to happen, despite overwhelming evidence to the contrary. This error causes anticipatory anxiety, which is normally much more upsetting to you than what actually ends up happening.*

An example of Jumping To Conclusions would be my thinking, "Our vacation is going to be miserable because it will be impossible to go on hikes and enjoy them now that we have a baby." Certainly taking our baby on the hikes will present us with new challenges, but she will hardly make the hikes impossible. Besides we've seen other couples hiking with babies over the years and they seemed to be having a good time.

As it turned out, our daughter really enjoyed riding in the backpack and seeing all of the new things on our many hikes; our vacation was great!

Another example would be when I call my cousin Tom and he does not call me back, I Jump To The Conclusion "Tom must be upset with me." Maybe Tom is terribly busy and has not had time to return any of his calls. I get busy sometimes and forget to return all of my calls. As it turned out he never received my message...all that worrying was for nothing.

2) BLOWING THINGS OUT OF PROPORTION: *This is where you make a mountain out of a molehill by viewing situations or events as catastrophic or insufferable when in reality they are not. If you stop to examine the situation realistically, you will find that the situation is not nearly as awful as you first imagined or thought.*

An example of Blowing Things Out of Proportion would be my thinking, "I will never find someone else to love" when my girlfriend dumped me after two years of going out together. That's ridiculous. I met lots of girls I would have liked to have dated over those two years if I didn't already have a girlfriend. I'm sure I will meet plenty of loveable girls soon.

In reality it allowed me to date many more girls before settling down and turned out to be a blessing in disguise.

3) EXTREME THINKING: *This is where you see everything as completely good or completely bad. With this kind of thinking, unlike real life, nothing falls in the middle.*

An example of Extreme Thinking would be: "This book has to be a success or I'm a failure." Not only is that ridiculous, it discounts every single thing I have done in my entire life up to the point of this book coming out, as well as anything I could ever do in the future. If the book is not a success, then the book is not a success but that's it. It has nothing to do with all of the rest of the things I've done or will do in my life.

4) GLOBALISING: *This is where you take one instance and fiendishly turn it into a universal event that will occur over and over again.*

An example of Globalising would be: I had one bad night of sleep and I had the thought, "I can't get a good night of sleep anymore." It's true that I did not sleep well last night but that does not mean that I am suddenly incapable of getting a good night's sleep. All it means is that I had one bad night of sleep. It was indeed an aberration and not indicative of a future of sleepless nights, though they do still happen on occasion, which is perfectly normal.

Other common thinking errors people make are:

1) EMOTIONAL BLOCKING: *This is where you give your feelings overriding importance. Just because you feel a certain way does not make it reality. Remember when I said, "Thoughts are not facts?" Well, all feelings come from your thoughts, so if your thoughts are inaccurate then your feelings are too. This often blocks your motivation in the form of "I don't feel like doing blank" so you don't.*

45

An example of this would be: "I don't feel like cleaning up my room right now." Of course, I don't feel like cleaning my room right now because when I think about cleaning my room it is overwhelming to me and seems like it will take forever. As a result of those thoughts I have about it, I don't feel like cleaning it right now and I never will feel like it if I continue to have those same thoughts about it. Conversely, if cleaning my room brought the following thought into my head: "Mom always gives me ice cream for dessert when I clean my room. I would really like some ice cream and cleaning my room only takes a few minutes," I would likely feel energized and be eager to clean my room.

2) REALITY FILTER: *This is where you zero in on one negative detail at the expense of not seeing the rest of the picture.*

An example of reality filter would be: I worked a gardening job all day pruning over 250 rose bushes and as I was finishing up the last one I accidentally cut off a few rose-buds I didn't see so "I concluded that I was a failure." Just because I cut off a couple of rosebuds on one bush, does not eliminate the fine job of pruning I have just completed.

My boss was thrilled with the good job I had done.

3) IGNORING THE POSITIVE: *You stubbornly refuse to give yourself credit for any of your accomplishments by telling yourself "Anyone could have done that" or "I just got lucky" every time you succeed.*

An example of Ignoring The Positive would be: People are always coming up to me and thanking me for my advice and telling me how I have helped them and how much they appreciate it. My reaction a few years ago would have been "I'm just fooling them; if they knew the real me they would not be so kind and appreciative." As if there was a little devil living inside of me. The fact was, I was helpful and they appreciated it. I was the only one discounting my work.

4) OMNIPOTENCE ERROR: *You think you are responsible for events that are clearly beyond your control.*

Here's an example of omnipotence error that I now find embarrassing, but was as real as could be to me at the time: I'm watching a college football Bowl game on Christmas day featuring my favorite team and player. They have the better team and I desperately want them to win. Things go miserably for my team from the start and despite the mercurial performance by my favorite player they come up just short in the end. I am furious and feel that it is my fault that they lost because I wanted them to win so badly. I even refuse to go with my wife to Christmas dinner at her aunt's house causing a huge fight with my wife. Needless to say, my wanting them to win – no matter how badly – had absolutely nothing to do with the outcome of the game. But at the time I was convinced that it was my fault.

5) COUNTERPRODUCTIVE MOTIVATION:

Instead of treating yourself with respect you try to motivate yourself using coercive language like "I should do this," "I have to do that," or to a lesser extent "I need to do this," as if you are obligated to do things. Using language like this makes any task seem onerous and will often leave you feeling guilty. When you think counterproductive motivational thoughts about others ("He needs to be more polite" or "She shouldn't be so prissy") all this does is make YOU more upset and frustrated.

An example of counterproductive motivation would be: "I have to mow the lawn." If you just change this to, "I will feel better if I mow the lawn," it would not cut into your self-esteem and you might feel more motivated to mow the lawn; nobody likes to be coerced or guilt tripped into doing things...Especially by themselves!

An example of thinking counterproductive thoughts about others is when you think, "They should have been more appreciative." In this way you are trying to force your values onto someone else. They may not share the same values and all you are accomplishing by doing this is upsetting yourself.

6) NAMING: *You put a name or label on yourself or others when a mistake is made or your performance falls short of perfect, such as saying, "I'm a loser" when you miss a deadline, or calling someone a "jerk" for cutting you off in traffic.*

For example: I went to the store to get a loaf of bread and as I was standing in line I realized that I forgot my wallet and thought, "I'm an idiot." Not only am I not an idiot, all I did was forget my wallet, nothing more and nothing less. Calling myself an idiot just makes me feel needlessly miserable on the way home to get my wallet.

If you are in the habit of attaching negative labels to yourself, you may also want to ask yourself what your definition of these labels are? For most of my life I was under the false impression that I was a "bad person" and "rotten to the core." It was only when I got these thoughts out of my head and exposed them to the light of day that I was able to see I had been needlessly torturing myself with these absurd notions.

This is the actual dialog I had with myself when I put this label to the test:

What is a bad person? "Someone who is rotten to the core." Describe what someone being "rotten to the core" means to you?

"It means you are always doing bad things. You don't care about anyone or anything and are extremely selfish. You have no conscience. Given the choice of doing good or bad, you will always choose bad. You have no redeeming qualities."

If you look closely at my answer, it becomes clear that not even Hannibal Lecter would live up to my definition of a person who is rotten to the core. So why was I torturing myself with these beliefs? Because I blindly accepted them as a child and never even thought to challenge them.

After I answered those questions I then asked myself: Does this definition sound like me?

"Not at all! I have always strived for goodness. If anything I'm full of goodness and caring. Just because my dad refused to see this and labeled me as being bad does not mean that it was ever true."

I was actually surprised to see that it did not look like me at all. I had spent the majority of my life believing something that had absolutely no merit at all. I was convinced that I was this horrible person and had to use all my energy to hide my badness from people. When in fact, this label was arbitrary and meaningless. This label/belief was incapacitating as it made me believe that life was hopeless, as no matter how much good I did, it would never change the fact that I was in essence a bad person. The folly in my belief of this label is so obvious now, but it never once occurred to me to question it. What labels were attached to you growing up that you blindly accepted like I did with this one? It's time to put them all to this simple test so you too can stop experiencing all the unnecessary anguish you've been putting yourself through.

Chapter Summary: Chances are high that you have been making more than one of these errors in thinking for some time. Some of you may be making all of these errors like I was. Now that you know what the most common thinking errors are, it is vital that you study these and begin to be on the lookout for them in your daily thoughts. In the next chapter I will present you with specific exercises for noticing these disruptive thought patterns, so that you can begin to refute them as you have them. I suspect you will be surprised how often you find them especially when you are feeling troubled or blue. Re-read the list of these thinking errors often, as the better you know them the faster you will be able to give yourself relief. I still review them regularly to this day.

Chapter
8

The Two Most Freeing Words

Now that you know the most common thinking errors it's time for you to try and spot them when you are making them so you can refute them. Before I get into specific exercises I want to share a little tip with you that Matt shared with me that proved invaluable. From now on, when something upsets you. I want you to get in the habit of saying/asking yourself, "So what?"

What you may not realize is that no one else and no event, no matter how catastrophic, has the power to upset you. It's the thoughts you have about it that upset you. That's why different people react much differently to the same event. Saying "So what?" gives you the chance to step back and look at

things more objectively. Many of ⸱
with negative thoughts (also calle
ic thoughts") that are activated b
uations but have no validity to⸱

My father was very harsh and I wa⸳ ⸳⸳
big trouble for any error I made no matter
how trivial it was. As a result I was trained to
react harshly upon myself whenever I made
ANY error years after he was gone. Here's
just one personal example of how poorly I
treated myself without being at all aware of
what I was doing:

Several years ago a friend of mine drove
a nice promotional vehicle for the company
he worked for and often left it with me to
store and use for short periods of time when
he was away. Needless to say I always took
good care of it and used it sparingly, but one
night I filled it up with gas and left the gas
cap behind. When I realized what I had done
I hurried back to the gas station in hopes of
retrieving it to no avail. All the while I was
beating myself up with such thoughts as
"How could I be so careless?", "What an idiot
I am!", "Chris is gonna be pissed and feel let

wn by me." You can just imagine how hor-
ible and small I felt thinking all those
thoughts and more. When I got home I called
Chris to tell him what had happened and
much to my surprise Chris's reaction was
"Oh hell, I've lost a couple of those. It's just a
standard gas cap that costs $5.00 and you
can get it anywhere." I was literally expecting
Chris to hate me forever for this one lapse
despite the fact we'd been friends since childhood. It never even occurred to me to say, "So
what?" I went through several hours of
anguish for nothing.

You may be surprised how often you
can short-circuit your negative automatic
thoughts just by saying "So what?" and
answering that question. Here's another
example from my life a few years ago just
after Matt shared the secret of saying "So
what?": I went to my post office box to get
the mail one Saturday morning and I found a
letter from the DMV informing me that my
license was scheduled to be suspended in ten
days because I was involved in an accident
and didn't have proof of insurance. Well I did

have insurance and showed proof of it at the scene. My first thoughts were, "that's just my luck, this sort of stuff always happens to me. It's like there's a cloud over my head." I began to get really upset and was about to start falling into the trap of playing the martyr and bemoaning to everyone how unfair it was etc. etc. Suddenly Matt's words took hold of me for the first time and I realized what I was doing. Then I thought to myself, So what? I can't do anything about it until Monday, so why am I compelled to let it ruin my weekend? I began to see how my martyrdom would only make ME feel worse and I was the one who always did that to me. I was amazed at how easy it was to not tell anyone about it and just let it go until Monday. I wondered how something so simple could change my mood so drastically? It was after this event that my progress accelerated by leaps and bounds. I got the glimmer of hope I had always been looking for and that enabled me to tackle the exercise I mentioned earlier that I had been struggling with. Oh yeah, and I cleared up the misunderstanding with the DMV in a surprisingly pleasant five minute phone call that Monday morning.

Chapter
9

The Holy Grail

The Thought-Error-Analysis or TEA Form (also known as the Thought Tracking Form), in my opinion, is the most important element of the Empowering Tools of Change.

It is a wonderful tool that only requires a pen or pencil and a piece of paper for you to do. You simply draw two vertical lines on a piece of paper and label the first column Thought (or thoughts). The second narrower column, you label Error(s), and the final large column, you label Analysis or Answer (an example of the TEA Form is shown on the following page Figure 9-1).

Let's say I am sent to the store to get some screws. I return with the wrong screws and I think the following thoughts, "I always

Figure 9-1

Thought-Error-Analysis or TEA FORM

THOUGHT	ERROR	ANALYSIS
The TEA-Form exercise won't help me.	Jumping To Conclusions	I won't know until I try it. If it does work I will be very grateful to have it available to me.
It (the TEA-Form) will be too difficult to do.	Jumping To Conclusions, Emotional Blocking	It feels this way because I'm overwhelming myself with negative thoughts. Things are rarely as difficult as they appear to be (to me) in my head.
I won't do it right.	Extreme Thinking, Jumping To Conclusions	I don't have to do it "right." It's a process and just like everything in life that you do, you don't do everything "right" the first time you try but you learn and adjust and get better at it over time. I didn't ride a bike "right" the first time I tried, but now I don't even have to think about what I'm doing when I ride a bike and this will likely turn out that way too, if I just keep repeating this exercise.
I'm not very good at stuff like this.	Globalising, Reality Filter, Naming, Jumping To Conclusions	Now I'm just making excuses to keep from trying this. No wonder I don't want to try with all those negative thoughts swirling around in my head. The sooner I get to work on this exercise the sooner all those irrational thoughts will disappear and I will begin to feel better. Once I get started, the exercise will likely become easier to do, but I'll never find out if I don't try it. I can do most things when I put my mind to them.

mess up" and "I'm such an idiot." Now let's look at the first thought: "I always mess up." Put that under the first (Thought) column. Now can you guess which thinking error this is? It is Globalising. Now put that under the second (Error) column. Nobody messes up all the time. It may feel that way because of the thoughts you are thinking in your internal dialogue with yourself, but that's what we're here to change.

Now what can we put in the final Thought-Error-Analysis or (Analysis) column to argue and replace this thought? How about "That's ridiculous! I made a mistake but I do most things right."

Now let's look at the second thought: "I'm such an idiot." Put that in the Thought column. Which thinking error would you put in the Error column after this thought? If you said "Naming" you're correct, you could also add "Blowing Things Out Of Proportion" and "Extreme thinking" to the middle column as well. Now let's fill in the Analysis column with a new more productive thought. How about, "I'm not an idiot, I just made a mistake and people make mistakes all the time." Now, I can go back to the store and get the right screw without feeling like I just went 12-rounds with the heavyweight champ and be done with it and move on with my life.

Now remember, in the Analysis column you want to refute your inaccurate thought and replace it with a more accurate and less upsetting thought. Do not use the Analysis column to cheer yourself up or say something you do not believe. It must be objective, so as to recognize the truth in the situation, for it to work.

Here's an example of the wrong way to respond to a thought in the Analysis column. Let's say you're nervous about going to a social engagement and the thought "No one there will like me" pops into your head. You would write that down in the Thought column, then identify the thinking error in column two. In this case the thinking error would be "Jumping To Conclusions."

The following would be the wrong thing to put in the Analysis column. "The people at these functions are always boring anyway."

Instead of refuting your automatic thought you have just committed several more thinking errors: "Extreme Thinking" when you group all the people together as one, "Naming" when you call them boring, and "Jumping To Conclusions," the whole thought.

A proper response in Analysis column would be something along the lines of: "I'm generally well liked by most people so why should the people at this party respond to me any differently?"

Or "So what? If I'm not having a good time I can always leave."

It is also important NOT to write down how you are feeling in the Thought column. For example, let's say you burned dinner and are thinking "I feel awful." There is no way to refute this because the fact is you do feel awful. However the thought behind your feeling awful –your thought in reaction to burning dinner – is refutable and it is what is making you feel awful. Perhaps the thought was "I'm a terrible cook." This is an example of "Extreme Thinking." Just because you ruined one meal does not take away the fact that you have prepared numerous wonderful meals.

As I stated earlier this seemingly simple exercise can be extremely difficult. I was terribly resistant to even trying it at first and would freeze up when I sat down to do it. Try and go easy on yourself and not be too critical of yourself on your early efforts. You didn't just wake up one morning and know how to drive a stick-shift. You had to work up to it and now you can do it without thinking about it. That's how this exercise works too.

If you are struggling with what to put in the Analysis or third column after you have written down your upsetting thought and the error in thinking, you may want to temporarily leave it blank and come back to it later or even show it to a friend or family member and ask them how they would respond to your thought.

I was warned early and often not to get stuck in the trap of doing this exercise in your head. For lasting results you need to snare all of your inaccurate thoughts on paper and refute and replace them with more accurate thoughts. However, I found it quite useful to practice doing this exercise in my head *in the beginning.* What that did was give me a glimmer of the possibilities for my improved mood through the use of this exercise. The problem is it can give you the false sense that you are doing enough just by doing it in your head; YOU AREN'T! You MUST do this on paper for lasting improvement. I try to spend 10-20 minutes a few times a week doing the TEA form exercise to this day.

Chapter
10

Putting Things Back Into Perspective

What is in your head is worse than anything you will likely ever experience. Most of the anguish you put yourself through comes from your distorted way of thinking about the things that happen to you. People who tend to be anxious or depressed often harangue themselves needlessly when something goes wrong.

Do you recognize yourself in any of the following examples? Your car breaks down on the way to work and you think "I knew I should have taken my car into the shop for a tune-up" or "This is just my luck." Neither one of these thoughts make the situation any better. All they do is place the blame for what happened on you and make you feel lousy. Consider the difference if you would have instead thought, "These things happen" and called for help. In either case you would probably need to call for help, but in the second example you accept that these things happen and deal with the problem at hand as opposed to beating yourself up for no good reason. Either way you will be on your way in the same amount of time so why make yourself miserable? The answer is because that's how you have always reacted in situations such as this. All you need to do is change your bad thinking habits that serve no useful purpose, and in time you will be feeling better about yourself and about life in general.

What if in that same situation you were going to miss an important meeting as a result of your car breaking down? Chances are you would also be having thoughts like "Now everyone is going to see how irresponsible I am" or "They're never going to entrust me with responsibility again" or "They'll probably fire me" or "There goes that raise I was hoping for." When you are overwhelmed with catastrophic thoughts like these you need to put things back into perspective by exposing those thoughts to reality.

You can do this by asking yourself what is the worst thing that would happen if your fears were realized? Then ask yourself what you would do? How could/would you cope? Try and get to the deepest fear in your head by starting with the first thought (for example: "They're going to fire me" and say to yourself, "Suppose they do fire me what would that mean to me?" Perhaps your answer would be "That I'm undependable." Then continue asking what that means to YOU until you get to the root of your troubling thoughts. What does being undependable mean to you? "That I'm not a good person." What does not being a good person mean to you? "That nobody will ever love me." What does no one ever loving you mean to you? "That I will always be alone." So what you are really afraid of was ending up alone and the thought of being fired triggered all the thoughts in your head associated with ending up alone just because you are late for one meeting.

See how silly these things become once they are exposed to the light of day. But as long as you keep them hidden in your head they have a life of their own that is continuously reinforcing these negative beliefs without opposition. It is crucial to your recovery that you get these thoughts down on paper where you can challenge their validity.

Once you have found the deepest thought you can then put all of these thoughts to the test using the TEA form. Now let's challenge all of the thoughts along the road to that deepest thought, starting with the first one, "They are going to fire me." In the Error column you would put "Jumping To Conclusions" and in the Analysis column we could refute this by saying "This is not the first time someone has been late to a meeting and I can't recall anyone else being fired just for being late to a meeting. Besides it's not like I missed it on purpose. My car broke down, I'm sure others have had car trouble before and will realize that getting to the meeting on time was beyond my control."

Now move on to the next negative thought that was in your head, "I'm undependable." Now put "Globalising" in the Error column and refute it in the third by saying: "That's ridiculous, I am more dependable than most of my co-workers. In fact, during my last review my boss commented on how much he appreciated always being able to count on me."

Number three "I'm not a good person." In the Error column put "Naming" and refute it in the Analysis column: "That's not true. I go out of my way to help out others when I'm able and if I was such a bad person no one would like me and I have lots of friends."

Number four "No one will ever love me." In The Error column put "Jumping To Conclusions" and refute this in the Analysis column by saying, "I have been loved before so it is entirely likely that I will be loved again; it may not be as much or as often as I'd like but I'm certain I will be loved."

And finally "I will always be alone." Again put "Jumping To Conclusions" in the Error column. Now refute it in the Analysis column with, "Who am I to predict the future? Besides some of my happiest times have come when I was alone. There are many things I could involve myself in to keep from being alone if that were what I wanted."

As you can see we often have thought patterns in place that we are unaware of and that take on a life of their own. They generally have absolutely no relevance to what is going on in any particular situation, but until they are countered will continually make many experiences in life needlessly miserable for us. Step back from the situation and ask yourself if that negative thought was true, what is the worst thing that can happen? If you then counter all the thoughts you come up with, you will be able to take the sting out of nearly every situation you encounter.

Chapter
11

The Wrist Counter

The final component of the Empowering Tools of Change will require you to go out and buy a simple wrist counter, used most commonly (until now ☺) by golfers to keep track of all of their swings. They generally cost between 5 and 15 dollars, and have a button you push that advances the number shown, by one, each time you push it. They can be found at sporting goods stores or golf shops and many of today's watches (such as Nike's line) come with a counter feature built-into them.

There are two different very simple exercises you can do with the wrist counter that I think you will find useful. The first is to count the number of negative thoughts you have about yourself each day. Every time a negative thought crosses your mind push the button on your counter. At the end of the day, write down how many of your negative thoughts about yourself you caught that day.

In the beginning you may only catch a few, but each day as you get better at recognizing when you're having negative thoughts about yourself you will see the number begin to rise. Don't be alarmed as this does not mean you're getting worse or messing up more. You are simply getting better at catching the thoughts which are causing you pain.

Remember it is crucial for you to begin catching these negative thoughts so that you can write them down and counter them with rational responses on paper using the TEA Form. I can't emphasize enough that the more thoughts you catch and counter the faster you will feel relief. Eventually the number of negative thoughts you are having about yourself will hit a plateau and then begin to fall. This is a good sign as it shows that you are beginning to exercise your self-control and that you will start to feel much better.

When I was having such a hard time getting started on the TEA Form this method helped me get better at recognizing when I was thinking the negative thoughts and enabled me to start snaring a few of them on paper. The more you do all of these exercises the easier they become and the faster they will begin to affect your moods.

While the most important ingredient of the Empowering Tools of Change is the writing down and challenging of your negative thoughts on the TEA Form, you do not need to write down all of the negative thoughts that you click off on the counter, but if you feel inclined to do so go ahead. This exercise is designed to supplement and or help you get started on the TEA Form.

Another equally simple and amazingly effective exercise you can use your wrist counter for is counting all of the things you do. This is especially helpful for perfectionists like me, or those who had parents who tended to focus on what they didn't do as opposed to what they did do. No matter what I did growing up my father always focused on what I didn't do. "Dad, I mowed the lawn and washed the car." To which he would respond, "Did you water the roses?" "Dad, I got four A's and a B on my report card" to which he'd reply, "Why didn't you get all A's?" etc. etc.

If you know the feeling, chances are you treat yourself the same way. No matter how much you accomplish, you always focus on what you didn't get done. This is not only very hurtful to you, but also serves no useful purpose. It probably has never even occurred to you that you do most things well. That's where this exercise is useful. Your lack of a sense of accomplishment will pale miserably compared to what you do accomplish once you begin to focus on all of the things that you do.

Why not give it a try for a few weeks? Just like in the other exercise, push the button on your wrist counter every time you do something. It can be anything, brushing your teeth, driving to work, smiling at someone, or even taking out the trash. At the end of the day write down the number of deeds you accomplished and track your progress. Soon you will see how much you do each day and will begin to harangue yourself less about what you don't get done.

Like I was with all of the Empowering Tools of Change when I first learned about them, I was incredulous to the idea that this would be helpful. But you know what? I was even more appreciative when I saw how well and easily it worked for me as well as others I know who have used this technique. I use this one all the time! Whenever I am a little down I put my wrist counter on and I'm always amazed at how quickly I begin to feel better; in fact I'm using it today as I write this.

Chapter
12

Helping Yourself

Now you have all the tools you need to get started on your road to recovery. Regardless of whether you just need some fine tuning, or a complete overhaul to the way you think about things, these tools will help you begin to enjoy life more. You will likely be amazed at how quickly these simplistic tools will begin to help your mood.

Best of all, you will be in control of both the speed and amount of your progress. The more you practice using The Empowering Tools of Change the greater the rewards will be.

The light switch...

For me living with anxiety and depression evolved into a situation where after seeing many different psychiatrists and psychologists, I gained much insight about what caused me to feel the way I was feeling, but very few means or tools to deal with how I was feeling and make it better. My quality of life had improved slightly. It changed from where I was able to walk into a dark room unable to find the light switch, to walking into a dark room and finding the light switch, but being unable to turn on the switch. Once I had the Empowering Tools of Change I was able to walk into the dark room, see the light switch, and turn it on for the first time in my life. And better yet, it became easier and easier to do each time I walked into the dark room of thoughts that used to dominate my mind.

Now it's time for you to start flipping all the light switches in your life. Good luck and enjoy the journey.

Section III

Un Poquito Mas

The final section of this book is intended for those who have suffered more severe depression, possibly due to physical abuse. It still may be worth looking at for everyone though. I strongly recommend that everyone read the final chapter on roller coasters.

Chapter
13

Good Will Hunting

If you have not seen the movie Good Will Hunting, I suggest that you rent it prior to reading this chapter. I don't want to give too much away about the movie but it focuses on the relationship between a boy (Will Hunting) and his therapist (Sean). Many have found this film tremendously helpful to them in their recovery, because like many who have had difficult upbringings they felt very alone in their predicament. This movie not only gave me the comfort of knowing I was not alone, it also gave me hope that it was possible to achieve significant recovery after growing up in a dysfunctional family.

I was surprised by how many of my friends and former teachers etc. saw aspects of my personality in the character of the movie's title role. I immediately saw the resemblance when looking back on my life at a similar age, but assumed I had hidden these aspects from others all along. At first I was genuinely shocked that I had not succeeded in my attempts at camouflage and at the same time I felt a little threatened by this realization. But then it began to become a source of strength in me as I finally realized that I no longer needed to be consumed with hiding my past. It made me realize that all these people I had failed to fool, liked me in spite of my upbringing. All my life up to that point (and even beyond to a lesser degree) I was ashamed and felt responsible for what had happened to me as a child. It had never dawned on me for even an instant that it was not my fault until I saw this movie.

Once I realized this, I hoped that everyone had seen through me and spotted me in the character Will Hunting in this movie. I felt a sense of relief about being myself. But much to my consternation and disappointment, I soon learned that I had hidden my past completely from many of the people I previously tried to be close to. These were the people I thought knew me better than anyone. These people liked what I was putting out in the world for consumption rather than liking the real me. It made me feel very empty inside when this realization hit me. I was especially sad when I found out I had fooled an old girlfriend who was an important part of my life, as well as one of my best friends.

The most disturbing and disheartening thing to me to come out of this movie was when I asked a friend who I respect, and is a successful film writer, what he thought of this movie. When he replied "I didn't like it. I mean come on, like a guy saying 'it's not your fault' is going to make him breakdown and get better just like that."

I was shocked. That one line, and the way in which it was repeatedly and insistently delivered cut right to the heart of what had been troubling me (and I'm certain a great many others) all of my life. I was unaware, until I heard it in this film, that those words were what I needed to be told. But even if anyone had ever tried to tell me this (and perhaps someone had?) I would not have heard it, as I would have always used my quick wit to change the subject and get the onus off of me (just like the movie character Will Hunting did all through this movie).

The difference in the movie was not just that it was 'the right words,' simple and easy to digest. But that the character Sean (the psychologist expertly played by Robin Williams) had a similar upbringing and knew from personal experience that the only way to get through to Will was to force the issue unwaveringly until it got through. The character Sean was unlike anyone Will Hunting or I had ever encountered; it was like finally meeting your match.

I sobbed like a baby when I saw that scene the first time and still sob every time I see it. I wish someone would have had the fortitude and experience/knowledge to have done that for me a long time ago. Unfortunately most therapists do not have this type of background and/or the savvy to know when and how to do this for their patients. In order for this to be successful a therapist would first have to develop a large measure of trust in their patient. This line delivered the same way earlier in the movie would have fallen on deaf ears. It was Will's trust in Sean that disarmed Will and enabled Sean to get through to him. Though I wished someone would have done this for me, I probably never trusted anyone enough for it to have been possible.

Hearing my friend dismiss the truest words in the movie made me realize how much ignorance exists in the world in regards to people that have been physically and/or emotionally abused. Often times abused individuals are misunderstood, but they are also often their own worst enemies, as they have a natural tendency to resist help, without realizing they are doing so, even while seeking help for themselves. It can be quite a daunting task, but they must learn to trust before they can overcome their problems. I'm hoping that hearing this from someone who has gone through this will make it easier for you to trust the methods I have recommended/outlined in this book.

I also want to mention one other very significant event that happened as I began my road to recovery. I received a call from a girl named Monica who was going to administer the Behavioral Assessment Tests (BATS) that each group member had to undergo prior to the start of our group. Once we scheduled a time to meet up for the BATS we continued talking and Monica asked quite a few questions about me. At one point in the conversation, I was talking about my oldest nephew who I often described as a younger version of me without all of the baggage. As I was talking about him Monica pointed out that I was talking as though I were already dead.

This revelation floored me as I had no idea that I was doing this. It also dawned on me that I had probably been doing this for months, if not years. Suddenly I saw myself as having transformed from identifying with the character Will Hunting into identifying with the character Sean who had grown dead inside prior to meeting up with Will. This shook me and made me realize I had given up. This insight gave me hope and even spurred me to go back and look at a book I had almost completed writing five years ago and had not looked at since then. It was the beginning of my true road to freedom and living and it was a great starting point for me to enter our group.

Chapter
14

What it Was Like to be Me

The following is an actual journal entry of mine before I was equipped with the Empowering Tools of Change. At its conclusion I will counter these thoughts using the tools outlined in this book.

A day in the life:
October 22, 1997 at 4:00am

I woke up with another mini anxiety attack. About two hours after going to sleep again. Went to the bathroom and tried to get back to sleep. Frustrated and filled with bothersome thoughts... Why does this keep happening? What can I do to make it stop happening? Why can't I just go back to sleep? I keep doing my breathing exercises to relax but they're not really helping. I felt short of breath again which in turn made me more anxious. I'm depressed and hate this helpless feeling. Why is sleeping so hard recently? I start to wonder and worry about if I have cancer and it's spread to my lungs whenever this happens and I'm short of breath. This only makes me more depressed. I start to think that maybe if I was back on Tofranil or on a higher dose of desipramine I'd be able to sleep through the nights again but I'm terribly torn as soon as these thoughts come to my head they are just as bothersome as they are soothing; on the one hand, right now I'm desperate for both sleep and desperate to get rid of all of these depressing thoughts but as soon as I come up with a solution that involves more medication, I become obsessed with avoiding the side effects, especially the ones involving my heart (beating faster and losing even more endurance). I even get so desperate that for brief instances trying drugs in the Prozac family even seem worth another try. For this I have even greater fear as the closest I've ever come to suicide was just after coming off of Prozac and that lasted for weeks and I've never felt fully recovered. I try and think about all of the things we've discussed related to these panic attacks/insomnia, looking for something to relieve the pain and desperation I'm currently feeling. But it's not working. Mainly, I think about wanting to end the pain and suicide starts to look like the only option. I constantly remind myself of all of the good feelings I've felt recently and long to feel them right now. I worry because even the recent good thoughts seem to be bringing me less and less comfort. Shawna (my wife) is awake with me right now and upon learning of these feelings I'm having and wanting to help she asked me if I was thinking about the natural alternative such as St. John's Wort to which I respond those thoughts have not come to mind at this time though I've thought about them many times before. I can see the concern and worry on Shawna's face and in her voice. It brings up many thoughts and feelings inside of me; wow, she really cares but I still feel bad although some of my thoughts are directed towards comforting and making her feel better which unlike comforting myself, I know I can do. When I see her like this it bothers me and I feel bad. It's amazing how the feelings I'm feeling in general close out the rest of the world and consume me with thoughts and hopes of getting away from these feelings and never wanting to ever feel them again. In this state of mind it is easy to become selfish and as blind to your actions effects on others, as others are kept blind to my feelings and what I'm going through.

It's unbelievably frustrating for me not to be able to sleep, even for the many years before I had any idea that I suffered from depression, etc. one thing from my teenage years on, I could always do well was sleep. In fact, I was often ridiculed for sleeping too much. Why can't I sleep anymore? I never imagined I would ever have trouble sleeping. Just like I never imagined that I would ever get fat or lose my hair. Those were the few things I always had to comfort myself. A few years ago I started losing my hair now I can't sleep. What's next? Losing my mind? Getting

Alzheimer's like my dad? Am I going to lose the few things left in my life that I thought that I could count on too? When I have thoughts like this, suicide becomes even more attractive and I have these thoughts a lot. If I leave now, maybe people would remember the good attributes I possess rather than waiting for all of them to disappear. I've always felt like an underachiever, which is bad enough, but these feelings of being an underachiever who's going downhill fast are terrifying. Why me? Why always me? I hate feeling sorry for myself. I hate being such a wimp. I try and tell myself just get over it but it's not as easy as it seems and seems to be getting harder every day. I remember the days growing up when I had no choice but to hold everything in and hide my every feeling from everyone. Sure I got sick all the time and was pretty miserable but at least I didn't know that there was any other way to be back then. I've had a taste of what feeling good or even just feeling feels like now and it makes it that much harder to bear putting up with all of these awful feelings. I used to look to the future to gain relief from the pain I was feeling but now I'm starting to feel like the future is in the past.

I'm tired and I need my sleep. I want to go back to sleep right now. I feel like time is slipping away from me. Yet I'm scared of all the thoughts that will start circling in my head when I try. I feel like I'm back on defense all the time in a different way than when I was growing up but all too much the same. It's no way to live. I think about things I want to do and no sooner than a thought comes into my head a fear comes in right behind it. Sometimes I think living like this is hell. How could it be any worse? I think I want to go visit somebody then I immediately think I can't because I may have an anxiety attack. How would you like to live where all your hopes and dreams are batted down by the fears inside your head and body before you get a chance to even try them? That's my life in a nutshell and I hate it. I'm going to try to go back to sleep now.

Obviously this was long before I had The Empowering Tools of Change. In retrospect it is easy to see that "my thoughts" were the cause of my pain and suffering that night. Now I am going to counter several of the thoughts in Figure 14-1 (on the following page) to show you how I could have dealt with those thoughts more effectively. All of those thoughts seem so silly now, but they could not have been more real to me at the time.

Figure 14-1

THOUGHT	ERROR	ANALYSIS
I have cancer and it has spread to my lungs; that's why I'm short of breath.	Jumping To Conclusions, Blowing Things Out Of Proportion	I have had shortness of breath off and on for a good portion of my life and it has never been diagnosed as lung cancer before, so it's highly likely that it is not lung cancer this time.
I'll get worse and become more suicidal and be more likely to act on my thoughts if I try another one of the Prozac family of medications.	Globalising, Reality Filter, Jumping To Conclusions	Just because I had a negative experience when I was briefly on Prozac does not mean I will react exactly the same way to all of the other drugs in that family of antidepressants. Perhaps that's precisely why there are so many different ones, because people react differently to them. It is also quite possible that my bad experience on Prozac could have been coincidental and had nothing to do with the medication. It's ridiculous to close off my options and make decisions based solely on one perceived bad experience.
I'm able to comfort Shawna but not myself.	Reality Filter, Ignoring the Positive, Extreme Thinking, Blowing Things Out Of Proportion, and Jumping To Conclusions	What was I doing before Shawna woke up? I was comforting myself by writing how I was feeling down. So I am able to comfort myself.

Chapter
15

Suicidal Thoughts

Trying to explain suicidal thoughts to someone who has never had them.

I got into a long talk with one of my closest friends when she expressed her exasperation and disgust with a friend of hers who tried committing suicide when they were just out of college. I shocked this friend when I shared with her how troubled I have always been with my own thoughts of suicide. Despite how close we were, the thought of me being suicidal had never crossed her mind. This particular friend is very bright, perceptive, caring and empathetic, but despite all of those traits she could not even fathom how someone could even consider committing suicide. She argued with me for hours bringing up points like how could you ever do this to me, or your wife, or your friends etc. She asked me how I could ever contemplate something so drastic when it would cause so much pain to all of the people I care about? She brought up many great logical arguments against suicide and I bought into all of her points. The problem was that there is not a lot of logic involved in suicide. I have been scared to death of dying since my mother died of cancer when I was a child. Now try and find the logic in the fact I have feared dying since I was a child and had suicidal thoughts shortly thereafter as well. There isn't any logic in that and therein lies the problem. I have always known I do not want to commit suicide. What scares me is that I know it only takes an instant to do and I have been close to that point on several occasions. I can picture myself jumping off a building and as soon as my feet leave the building saying to myself, "What the hell am I doing?" but by then it would be too late. My friend really forced me to come up with a way of showing her the mindset of someone who is contemplating suicide. It took a lot of thought and effort and the best explanation I could come up with was this:

Think about sometime when you were really having a bad day. One where you were getting bombarded with things to do at home or at work and were completely overwhelmed, where you felt like you needed to get away and get some coffee or fresh air or something to keep from exploding or going crazy. Now at that moment when you reached the point you needed to step away for a few minutes, were you thinking about the effects of your stepping away on other people or were you totally consumed by the need to get away?

If you answered honestly you would admit that all you were thinking about at that moment was escaping*. That's what it is like to have suicidal thoughts, but the problem is that when you reach that point of needing to escape, what you need to get away

---

*= It is important to note that I am talking about the exact moment, a split second in time. Not even a second before (or after) when you still may have been consciously weighing your options.

from is not the office or your house or your kids, it's you and more specifically your mind. People that commit suicide don't have the capacity to think of the ramifications of their actions at that moment when they are consumed by their pain. When you are consumed by pain nothing else matters, you just want to get out of your pain as fast as you can. If a tree falls on top of you crushing your ribs, with no one around to help you, at the moment of impact are you more concerned with getting the tree off of you or the fact that you may upset your wife and friends for being late? We have all heard of the people that were stuck in seemingly hopeless situations who had to cut their own arm off to survive. Now do you think those people were thinking about all of the disadvantages of not having their arm or were they consumed by survival? On September 11th, 2001 in the aftermath of the two large airplanes crashing into the World Trade Center buildings many of us witnessed or saw pictures of people jumping from the upper floors of the two buildings to escape the fire engulfing the buildings. It's reasonable to assume most of these people were aware that the odds of surviving such a fall were virtually nil, but faced with certain slow and painful death by fire, the astronomically small chance of surviving the fall was the most appealing option they had.

Survival is one of human being's most basic instincts and supersedes all other thoughts when our survival instincts are activated. As illogical as this may sound, suicide is a survival mechanism. Yes, that's what I said. SUICIDE IS A SURVIVAL MECHANISM. More accurately, suicide is the survival mechanism run amok. The problem is that you are trying to survive that moment and in doing so you have paid with the loss of your life rather than, say, the loss of your arm as in the previous example. It all goes back to our most basic instinct of fight or flight. When the suicidal thoughts come most of us try and fight them with logic and diversion etc. When fighting does not work we naturally turn to flight and the only way to flee your mind is to shut it off, ergo suicide.

One final note...since I have been practicing the Empowering Tools of Change I have not had any thoughts of suicide, a remarkable change in and of itself for me! If you look closely at the thinking patterns of someone with suicidal thoughts it is not uncommon for them to be suffering from all ten of the thinking errors outlined in this book.

Chapter
16

Roller Coasters

There is something especially empowering about tackling something you fear head-on. I first came upon this realization on a trip to Six Flags Magic Mountain when I was in high school. I was with a bunch of my friends and as soon as we got out of the car and looked at the big roller coaster Colossus standing right before us, the first words out of my mouth were, "There's no (expletive) way I'm going on that!" You see, I was terrified of most rides and especially terrified of roller coasters and I don't just mean big ones; even the little ones you find at carnivals or county fairs.

Much to my surprise none of my friends reacted to my statement. I had expected the usual childhood taunts like, don't be a wimp etc. etc. but no one addressed my statement directly. Little did I know one of my friends (Anthony) had a plan to get me on Colossus before the day was over. Anthony started by getting me to go on the little starter roller coaster Gold Rush. I even protested pretty vociferously against getting on that one, but Anthony smartly said, "come-on it's not like I'm asking you to get on Colossus." So I figured I better ride that one, so I wouldn't have to ride Colossus.

I was pretty terrified at first, but actually kind of enjoyed some of the ride by the end of it. A little bit later Anthony suggested going on Revolution, which was a pretty big roller coaster with an upside down loop. I protested and Anthony teased me badly about how I was a big baby. Somehow they got me to ride it. Anthony laughed that once we got off Revolution, I was holding on so tightly that if the car left the track my hands never would have left the bar I was holding onto; and he was right. They would have had to pry my fingers off that bar.

Again, much to my surprise, once we got past the first terrifying drop, I began to get some enjoyment out of the ride. As the day was winding down we got over to Colossus and I again vociferously repeated that there was no way I was going on it. Anthony harassed me beyond any amount he had ever harassed me before, but I was as firm as I had ever been in my life. I was not getting on that roller coaster. Eventually everyone was on my case but I was not about to budge. Finally everyone but me went to ride on it and I waited for them by the exit. When they came off the ride I could see the thrill and excitement in their faces; especially my friend John Robertson's eyes. I had never seen him so pumped up and they all said they were going to ride it again.

Anthony somehow convinced me to at least go through the line with them and promised me I could leave at the chicken exit before they got on if I really did not want to go on it. They were selling me on the ride's virtues and trying to convince me there was nothing to be afraid of all through the hour-long line. I was reading all the precautionary signs; you know the ones that say, "if you are pregnant, have ever had any kind of heart problem, nervous disorder, back problem, or are not in good physical condition you should not ride this ride."

All I could think about were all the things that I imagined were wrong with me. My heart always beat at a faster resting pace than it should no matter how good of shape I was in, so I was CONVINCED there was something wrong with my heart that had never been detected. I was reasonably certain in my mind that I was going to die on the first drop of the ride if I got on it.

On top of that I had always been a nervous person growing up so it seemed entirely likely that I suffered from a nervous disorder as well. I never really had any back problems but my back had hurt before so maybe I did have back problems too. I was an athlete at the time, but I was not in top shape so perhaps I was not even in good physical condition. In fact the only warning I could dismiss for sure was that I was not pregnant.

It is hard to imagine anyone being more terrified of getting on that roller coaster than I was that day. I remember the scornful disgust from Anthony as I was about to chicken out, but I don't remember exactly what he said that got me into the car next to him that day. I wanted to escape more than anything else in the world and as the roller coaster reached the top of that first hill in the agonizingly slow climb that roller coasters always have, I thought I was going to freak out and lose control and make a spectacle of myself.

As the roller coaster went over the top and began to accelerate down the hill I grew more and more terrified in each millisecond. But just as we got a little over halfway down that first drop something miraculous happened to me. I was as terrified as is humanly possible, and I discovered that once you reach that point it does not get any worse. You've already reached the limit of your fear and all it can do at that point is lessen. No switch turned in my head to make me lose control and I didn't die. In fact not only did my fear lessen, it practically disappeared and turned out to be one of the best experiences I ever had.

I left with a confidence that I had not previously had; that I could conquer even my most terrifying fears if I was willing. Growing up in such a negative environment everything in my life had been based on fear and all my decisions were guided by which choice induced the least amount of fear in me. That is no way to live. The fact that my fears were such a big part of me at the time of my "conquering" of Colossus, I feared that my good experience on Colossus was a "fluke" and every time I ride a roller coaster to this day I still get a pang of fear that I have just been lucky and all my fear will come back and be justified. That first ride was over 20 years ago now and I have ridden a lot of roller coasters since then.

Just yesterday I went back to Six Flags Magic Mountain and rode their newest biggest and fastest roller coaster named Goliath. It starts with a 250 foot drop that goes directly into a dark tunnel at 85 miles per hour. The drop is nearly twice as long as the drop on Colossus and 25 miles an hour faster. I have to admit I was pretty intimidated by it and not sure I was going to have enough courage to board it when the day began.

Many people I know have told me that they can no longer ride roller coasters now that they are "older" and many of these people are barely in their thirties. I was nearly 40 at the time and had not been on a roller coaster in over a year and the thought occurred to me that perhaps I was getting too old to ride the larger roller coasters. A thought that seemed even more convincing after starting the day on the relatively tame Revolution and coming away from it feeling rather wobbly.

My friend John and I really had to convince each other to give Goliath a try. As we got into the line I immediately noticed that the warnings for this roller coaster were more stringent than those for Colossus and the other roller coasters we had ridden at the park. In addition to the usual warnings about pregnant women, back trouble and nervous disorders, Goliath added warnings about being under the influence of alcohol or drugs as well as just having high blood pressure. I don't think I have ever been able to board a new big roller coaster without sending my blood pressure soaring!

I was almost as terrified of going on this roller coaster as I had been over twenty years earlier of going on Colossus. But there were two big differences in my mind and one was good and the other was bad. The bad one was that I was feeling vulnerable because of my age and because my blood pressure had been high recently, which brought back all of those old thoughts about being in serious physical danger and/or dying. I even reminded my wife where my Will was prior to getting in line. It did not help that very few people in line looked older than me.

The good difference was that I am now equipped with the new skills referred to in this book that help me put things back into perspective and alleviate many of the mostly unfounded fears I was feeling. Just using the

tools in this book allowed me to remain surprisingly calm all through the line despite my
many fears. I was pretty scared once we
boarded and it made its climb to the top, but
I resisted the urge to close my eyes as one
passenger had suggested. As I felt the pull
when we began our rapid descent I started to
feel the full effects of sheer terror when suddenly halfway down the drop I turned to my
friend and hollered "this is great!" I raised my
arms for the remainder of the ride and
deemed it the best roller coaster I have ever
experienced. The feeling of accomplishment
was almost as sweet as that first time I rode
on Colossus.

What was especially interesting about
this experience was the contrasting way that
my friend John and I were looking at our
impending ride on Goliath because he grew
up in the Cleaver family as opposed to the
dysfunctional family I grew up in. He was
apprehensive about going on Goliath but not
nearly as fearful as I was. Once we got in line
I knew he was not going to back out, but I

was not 100% certain that I would not chicken out.

As we talked about what we were thinking it was interesting to note that what he dreaded was how he expected he might feel after the ride, while I was terrified of the initial descent. I was confident that if I "*survived*" the initial drop I would enjoy the remainder of the ride. While he was looking forward to the drop and fearful of how his body would react to the forces of the corkscrew on the ride. While he feared how he would feel getting off of the ride, I was looking forward to the feeling of accomplishment of having completed the ride.

Over the years I have found several other things I was formerly afraid of and have used them to get that feeling of empowerment. I recommend that people try and do something they are afraid of (that is relatively safe) at least every few years to reinforce their confidence, as I have found that the effects almost always spill over into other areas of my life.

After-Word

Now that you have finished reading my book you have the tools you need to travel down the road to your bright future. Getting started is the hardest part of the journey. If you find yourself struggling with these tools – *as I was for the first month or so* – I suggest you arrange to meet with a professional trained in cognitive behavioral therapy (CBT) a few times to help get you going.

Once you are using the tools regularly you will be able to control the speed and depth of your progress. Simply put, the more you do the exercises the sooner you will begin to see results and the better you will become at giving yourself relief.

For those of you who feel you have mastered the tools in this book, I have listed additional resources that may be of additional help to you on the following page.

Remember, with the use of these tools you can change your future but not your past.

Enjoy the ride!

Additional Resources

Anxiety Disorders

Behavioral Research Program

Director: Professor Michelle G. Craske

Department of Psychology

405 Hilgard Ave.

Los Angeles, CA 90095-1563

•

Center for Anxiety and Related Disorders

at Boston University

648 Beacon Street, 6th Floor

Boston, MA 02215

www.bu.edu/anxiety

•

Feeling Good by David Burns M.D.

•

Learned Optimism by Martin Seligman

•

Dedication

I went to Maryland to spend Thanksgiving with my aunt and uncle's family soon after I graduated from college. I was picked up at the airport by my cousin Andy who I had not seen since I was three years old. He was a couple of years older than me and had grown up to be 6'8" tall. He was intense and gregarious but seemed a little awkward; I wrote that off as being a consequence of his being so tall. Andy was excited to see me and peppered me with questions about Los Angeles the entire time I was there. He talked longingly about possibly attending graduate school at USC the following fall.

Much to my surprise he got a job transfer and moved to Los Angeles a few months later. Since I had not come from a close family, it was nice to have a relative living close.

I introduced Andy to both of my roommates and we tried to help make his transition to living in LA as comfortable as possible. We enjoyed spending time with him and he seemed to like being in our company as well. Andy was always full of questions and he often got into spirited debates with one of my roommates and me. As I got to know Andy better I began to notice he was more reluctant to try new things than most people I knew. In short, he seemed a lot like me prior to my first ride on Colossus.

So when my roommates and I were planning a trip to Magic Mountain I tried very hard to convince Andy to go with us. I was convinced that the experience would prove as freeing for Andy as it was for me. Not only was he as adamant as I was about not riding Colossus, he had the resolve of someone much older and would not even go to the park with us, as he was convinced he would not enjoy it. I shared my experience so as to empathize with him and I was fairly relentless but in the end could not get Andy to go.

Several months later, without any warning signs that either I or my roommates picked up on, Andy tragically took his own life. I felt responsible for his death (Omnipotence error) for well over a decade. I even thought his parents blamed me for it (jumping to conclusions). I mean he'd gone most of his life without knowing me and had no problems I was aware of, and then less than a year after he moves out here by me he was dead. I still regret failing to get Andy on Colossus and I dedicate the chapter on Roller Coasters to him.

Notes

Super Tao Order Form

(All prices shown are in U.S. dollars)

Internet orders: **www.tao3.com**

Postal Orders: Super Tao, P.O. Box 1081, Manhattan Beach, CA 90267. Make checks payable to Super Tao, Inc.

Please send me _____ copies of "Been There, Done That? DO THIS!" at $12.95 each to:

Name: _____

Address: _____

City: _____

State:_____ ZIP:_____ Country_____

E-mail Address: _____

Sales tax: Please add 8.25% for all orders shipped to California addresses.

Shipping U.S.: $2.50 for first book and $1.00 for each additional book.

International: $8.00 for first book and $4.00 for each additional book.

Payment method: __Check __Money order

(Credit card please use web for your order)

http://www.tao3.com